Bread

U, or love a best wishes to a
treasured goddaughter

Bku

Dec 2021

Bread

Bread

My search for what really matters

Glenn Myers

Copyright © 2021 Glenn Myers
First published 2021 by Fizz Books
Version 0.9 (ARC)

Glennmyers.info

ISBN 978-0-9565010-9-7 (paperback)
ISBN (epub)

Cover design by Chris Lawrence

British Library Cataloguing in Publication Data
A CIP catalogue for this book is available from the British
Library

For my parents, who in more than sixty years together helped us see what really matters

CONTENTS

CONTENTS

START HERE

We should reckon on 30,000 days in our lifetimes – 82 years. After that (if even we get that far) we will find ourselves mostly filling our days fending off the Second Law of Thermodynamics. The Second Law of Thermodynamics roughly means everything breaks, nothing lasts, order breaks down, we're all going to die. Nothing in the Universe pushes back for long against the Second Law.

Thirty thousand days puts a cap on how many of anything we will do: how many books or boxsets we can enjoy, or create, how many cities we can live in, how many hot dinners we'll have. We've got one ration of weddings, birthdays, weekends away, meals out, drinks with friends, quiet nights in, or moments to tell someone we love them. We've got a few decades to serve in a career or two, and perhaps raise some children. It might feel it will go on forever. It won't, and in a hundred years we will be dust and so will those we love.

If you feel any of these:
- *Life is passing me by*
- *I'm not doing what I want to do*
- *I'm not happy*

- *I'm wasting my days*

This book is for you. I've kept it short, because, hey.

It's a personal story of discovery. My background is some years of life-and-death medical adventures, including my death in 2011 (reversed by electric shocks to the heart) and a four-week coma in 2013. People who spend a long time in Intensive Care end up paralyzed, so during the year and a half after 2013 I had to learn again how to eat, swallow, walk and go to the toilet. Eventually I put the wheelchair in the garage and resumed a life that feels, at the time of writing, restful, purposeful and happy. I still may have thousands of days unused if I'm, as my dad says, 'spared.'

Life is the opposite of the countryside in that you see the widest views at the lowest points. I think most people learn things about themselves during adversity. I had time to ask questions like 'What am I for?' and 'What am I hoping for?' and 'What am I spending my time on?'

I found answers that are good enough for me. I think they are the lessons everyone learns, but those of us who have been force-fed these things through medical events, perhaps, are forced to face them quicker. I found them simple enough and roughly these:

1. Suffering helps us focus on what really matters and can stop us heading down dead-end paths in the quest for fame, success or respect.
2. *Belonging* is key to long-term thriving.
3. So is *purpose*.

10

This book, then, is about how to simplify your life, and how to make you less restless, more content and more productive. I hope it helps. None of it is complicated. Some of it will happen to you anyway. Maybe this book will help you recognize and cooperate with the ripening and mellowing that is already underway in your life.

I am often suspicious of people who offer self-help, not least because of the sub-text that these people have now got their act together. This is not me. Nor have I put together a set of resources on the web, nor a 30-day nutrition guide to a new you, nor a set of videos for a reasonable price. I have too many chins to be a sleek self-help guru and would probably need to stand on a box for the publicity shot. I did really find something though and I hope that in the next 20,000 words you'll find something that works for you too.

There are three main parts to my presentation: *suffering*, *belonging*, *making*. The optional fourth part (*believing*) explains how the first three are taken to another level through my faith. Think of this final section as bonus material. You can skip it, but you'll miss out.

***

Back in the 18th century, in my country, the Royal Navy was the tentpole holding up the marquee of Britain's sudden prosperity. Naval inspectors realized, though, our ships were weak when they were built from unseasoned wood. They looked good, but they fell apart.

11

In an early instance of military industrial policy, and a notable example of competent procurement, they ordered that seasoning sheds be constructed that would be adequate for the Royal Navy's needs.

It was a big job. The one ship from that time that is still in commission is *HMS Victory*, Nelson's flagship. It was built from 6,000 oak trees. Each oak needed years in a seasoning shed. The naval inspectors' ambition was to store at least three years' worth of felled oak in sheds so that the naval dockyards could build everything they needed, even if there was a rush job because of a war, and all the time use seasoned timber. Soon the naval dockyards were surrounded by a vast stack of freshly-sawn oak, all facing the English weather, being seasoned into an unsurpassable building material for ships. Seasoning made them seaworthy. (Chatham Docks in the southeast corner of England is now a heritage site and you can visit the great navy-building machine that it became, including the seasoning sheds.)

I too have been seasoned by the forces of suffering, belonging and making. I think they season all of us. Many people, maybe you too, have been thoroughly seasoned through many harsh seasons. I am not sure if I am seaworthy yet. But perhaps we may be all seaworthy sooner if we realize what is going on and how we can use it.

Glenn Myers, Cambridge, 2021

www.glennmyers.info   www.slowmission.com

SUFFERING

In any crisis your body gives you an emergency shot of the panic juices. A course of fight-or-flight hormones may take you through a crash, or a hospital treatment, or a birth, or a breakup, or the funeral arrangements or whatever other intense time you must rise to.

Two things will then happen. You will have a bit of a tumble emotionally as the hormones leak away and normal tiredness takes over. And, second, because the intensity of the storm has passed, you can inspect your new world.

This season can be a blessing because it can give you a clear sight of what to do. It's like clearing up after a party. The mess! The stains in the carpet! What are you going to do? Time for the cleaning gloves.

I'm hoping that your dose of stress hormones wasn't too excessive or prolonged. There is good evidence that flooding your body again and again with this chemistry can lead to many health problems. It's especially bad when it happens to children. Extreme stress poisoning is not incurable, but it is not what I am writing about here. I'm talking about us ordinary people, who had decent childhoods and lives and maybe only now have been hit by some disaster or loss.

If you haven't been hit by some disaster or loss at all, all the better. When trouble comes, perhaps you'll be readier to make the best of it.

So. The house is quiet now, and there's a new post-trauma world to explore. What to do? Some thoughts:

You were broken already. You might feel that now you are wounded and before you were whole. I'm sorry to report that this picture is wrong. You might feel like a broken egg now, but you were never the whole egg. You were already cracked, back in the shop. All that's happened is that you've revised your mental model of yourself. You always were needy, but you used to cover it well.

Take time. You've done rushing for a bit. You can take some breaths, re-evaluate, start small.

Decide it's work time. You've already vaguely suspected there are things to sort out in your life, but the calamity brings them into the open. The singer Debbie Harry explained her drug-taking: 'Drugs aren't always about feeling good ... Many times they are about feeling less.'[1] True, but avoiding the pain with pharmaceutical assistance keeps forever dropping you back at the start, each time with a little more clearing up to do. You are made of better stuff.

Feel the fire. This is the best bit. There's a fire burning inside you. Still. This is so clichéd a thought that it may call song lyrics to your mind. *I will survive! There's something inside so strong!* It's probably best for everyone if you don't sing—you are not a rock star for a reason—but on the bright side you have discovered something about yourself. You will go on. You will push on. We humans didn't take

---

[1] Debbie Harry in her memoir *Face It*.

14

over the world because we're a species of wimpy losers. So the party's over and your home is wrecked? On we go. On we go. The cracks let the light in. The breaking is the start of the mending.

Where are we heading here?

Where are we heading? Towards a rethink. Convalescence after hospital nightmares gave me the moment, and the need, to shut down some old mental pathways and open some new ones. I sadly cannot declare final victory in this fight, but I do think that much of the time I have persuaded my brain to walk down a more promising road.

Suffering is our friend here. How do you see the new mental pathway that needs to be cut? That's the clarity of low mood. What powers the cutting of the path? The fire inside you and your determination to see a better day, or at least another day. How does the path become well-trodden and familiar? By you taking it, day after day after day. Facing adversity well, every day, sometimes every hour, builds a resilient brain. In the end you'll have carved a fresh path with many delights where you love to walk.

How do we do this?

Let's look more closely at a couple of sources of adversity and see the futile, directionless mental pathways to abandon and the purposeful good paths to tread down. As examples of adversity and loss I'll choose *failure* and *sudden infirmity*.

Failure and *infirmity* are different from each other and from other causes of adversity like pain, anxiety, divorce, bereavement, assault, betrayal, backstabbing, abuse, being stalked, being childless, being bullied, or being shot, for example, but they are all countries in the same region. Just like all hot countries have cockroaches and palm trees, so one person's life-altering adversity resonates with another's even if one has lost her baby and another has lost her trust in men. Hopefully looking at a couple of traumas in detail will give all of us something for any of the rest. So the next part of this book looks in detail first at failure and then at sudden infirmity.

Failure

Failure first. Failure's astonishingly common. Prime Ministers and Presidents feel it. Millionaires feel it because they are not billionaires. Maybe all of us feel it. Who hasn't felt a failure compared with a brother or sister? Who doesn't feel they have disappointed their parents?

Perhaps some people feel a failure *all the time*. What's it like to go to school knowing that you won't get it, that you are failing? Some of us were born into failing regions or into failing sociological groups or we had monstrous childhoods and we carry the baggage of that every day. We start behind in the race of life.

For others of us, failure is something that's never happened before and isn't in our background and shouldn't happen. You are probably too socially sensitive to say out loud 'How could I fail? I never fail!' You just did fail, though.

And for still others of us, we may be succeeding well in one area of life, but another area has crashed: like carrying lots of shopping and the bottom has fallen out of a single bag. This applies to people who, for example, are successful professionally but catastrophic domestically. It's a failure of integrity, of completeness. You look good, but know you aren't. Sometimes our domestic failures reach out like a crocodile and snap us away from our public successes too. Then we know we've crashed and burnt.

Failure also isn't fair. We quite like it when people who deserve to stumble and flail do so, but failure isn't quite that choosy, or quite that able to deliver poetic justice.

You can plan well and still fail

You can work hard and still fail.

You can be scrupulous not to fail and still fail.

You can 'leave everything out on the field' and fail.

You can believe that it is your *attitude* and not your *aptitude* that governs your *altitude* and still *fail and crash and burn* because the aphorism has yet to be written that can withstand a crunching collision with reality.

You might be angry about this. You are not one of those people who cut corners, tread on others, and don't care about their carbon footprint—an overweight, aggressive, insecure loser who absolutely deserved to fail. That's not you. Failure happens to lovely people who launch into good things with integrity and just the right amount of fear. You didn't get the job, or the boy, or the contract, or the grade, or the lasting relationship. Maybe in all sorts of ways it wasn't your fault exactly. But you didn't make it. I'm so sorry.

And what about something that you don't want to label 'failure' but you would label 'disappointing'? You got the job you craved, but the working environment thwarts you at every stage. You didn't fail, as such—you got the job—but you are disappointed and perhaps burning out. It isn't failure, but you may feel some of the same emotions as the rest of us reading this.

Anyway. Here you are, beached, in your one and only life, your 30,000 days ticking by. By whatever route, you have arrived at the destination called 'Failure,' or maybe the nearby stops of 'Disillusion' or 'Disappointment.' That dream: it's gone. I'm so sorry. But you've come to a good place. Now for the re-thinking, and now for the good health.

What's the main gift these circumstances can give you? You have believed false things about the world and your place in it. Failure, or one of those words beginning with 'dis-' crumbles these beliefs. Recovering, if you do it right, leads you to a more realistic and humbler place. The good thing about the new place is that you can find the contentment and personal worth you always wanted.

These lessons don't come in a neat package. Let's look at some of them individually and put them together later.

- We don't know much
- Bad stuff happens
- The top is crowded
- Time reveals the truth

We don't know much

I don't know if you've ever thought about how your parents launched you into the world, but whatever they supplied you with, it wasn't enough. Look at us. Little scraps of life teeming in the water-droplet that is the blue Earth, surrounded by giant fusion reactors—distant stars—that haven't passed a safety inspection. One ripple of instability in one of these, especially the nearest one, and we're all vapour. Look how little we know. We have sensors attached to the outside of our body, but they detect just glimpses of reality. We assemble these flashes into a mental model of the universe. We mistake the model in our head for the real universe all around us. We navigate the world with this flawed model. No wonder we crash.

What do we understand about people, the future, the past, even this day? What even do we know about simple things: what is a good life? What is a good end? What is a soul? Leaving school with a working knowledge of Pythagoras' Theorem and a 25m swimming certificate may not count as proper preparation. As young adults we are dumped on the shore of an alien world with no signposts – all of us. That feeling of successful invulnerability you always had? You were wrong. We're blind people in a world with jagged edges and discovering this was only a matter of time.

Bad stuff happens

Ancient Jewish wisdom describes that bad stuff happens:

> *The race is not to the swift*
> *or the battle to the strong,*
> *nor does food come to the wise*
> *or wealth to the brilliant*
> *or favour to the learned;*
> *but time and chance happen to them all.*

19

Moreover, no one knows when their hour
will come:

As fish are caught in a cruel net,
or birds are taken in a snare,
so people are trapped by evil times
that fall unexpectedly upon them.[2]

The universe has a habit of surprising us. You'll be striding proudly over a landscape (as I did in the English Lake District once) and step thigh-deep into a bog.

The real mystery is that we don't crash more often. Albert Einstein famously said that 'The eternal mystery of the world is its comprehensibility … The fact that it is comprehensible is a miracle.'[3] The Universe's stolid, Teutonic regularity, and the way science has opened some of its secrets, and material life has over the centuries got better and better, all blind us to the larger truth that we no more understand reality than a fly does, smashing against a window and wondering why the air has turned solid. To us the Universe is like a whale that swims below the surface, massive but safe, but then suddenly breaches, all its weight and bulk flying out of the water.

Or think of the turkeys that are grown on our local farm. The farmer feeds them. They grow up. They get on with the politics of the pecking order. People come to look at them and they waddle over to see them, gobbling with pleasure. In all the long history of the species *Meleagris*

---

[2] The book of Ecclesiastes 9:11-12
[3] *Journal of the Franklin Institute*, 1936, according to Andrew Robinson in *Nature* 30 April 2018, 'Did Einstein Really Say That?'

gallopavo domesticus, rarely has a flock been so healthy, so safe, so sleek. No-one has told them about Christmas. Are we like the turkeys? We think we have a handle on life but we have no idea what we are for, if we even are for something, or that an end awaits us that is entirely outside our collective experience and knowledge?

Failure teaches us not to be too surprised when bad things happen.

The top is crowded

A third lesson we may find is the phenomenon of limited good. We live in an era of abundance, but still there is a shortage of some good things, and not everyone can have them. The gorgeous human that would make a wonderful life partner is already taken.[4] Lots of things in life seem like pyramids, millions of us at the base, only one or two at the top. Footballers, musicians, writers, politicians: we can look fondly at those at the top of the pyramid, and we can even read how they got there, but that doesn't mean there's room for all of us. There isn't. This is another brute fact about the Universe.

J K Rowling and I both published a book in 1998. Hers was the first in the Harry Potter series; mine was a non-fiction account of the Arab World. I think my initial print run was larger than hers; but just that once. Prizes, wealth, success deservedly followed Jo Rowling. She's at the top of the pyramid and deserves to be. God bless her, a good person made good. I'm still at the base, and God bless me too. There is plenty of space down here for less-

---

[4] Sorry.

than-successful people to be not at the top of their chosen profession.

So: we know little, bad things happen, most of us don't win the race. We are people of limited knowledge, limited luck and limited access to the good. These are the marks of the poor; our marks. And if we're not wise enough to see them now, we'll learn them eventually.

The effect of time

The reason we will learn them eventually is because of the compounding effect of time.

You only need to live half a lifetime to know of people who once dominated headlines but die disappointed, frightened and alone; their future was obvious if only we could have worked out how their character and actions would ripen with time. The same is true of fashions, ideas and trends. Time exposes the shabbiness that a person or mass-movement wears under the celebrated exterior. Time also sorts the tortoises from the hares. Some people will live a good life no matter what time and chance do to them, because they are like that. Others, who may be famous or much followed, will collapse under the strains of time, because they are like that.

What survives the unravelling tug of time? The same things that failure can't strip away: the inner qualities of heart and character.

Our story so far

So to summarize lessons of failure or disappointment:

1. We are poor, not rich, not in control, not masters of our destiny.
2. The inner qualities of heart and character may be worth cultivating more than a celebrated exterior.

Infirmity

Now a second species of loss and adversity: infirmity. The day came once, perhaps when I learnt I had to take pills for the rest of my life, when I realized I was chronically sick. I felt like I had been tramping over a sunny landscape all my life, but at that moment I had wandered into a cave. Outside, somewhere else, the sun was still shining and the wind gusting and the sea crashing, but these elements were no longer shining, gusting or crashing for me and perhaps never would again. I had left the land of good health, and, I feared, happiness.

Yet there were treasures in the cave. And a cave of some kind is the only place to find them. A person who studies caves professionally is called a speleologist; in life, people aren't recruited into speleology, nor do they choose to go; they are press-ganged. Cancer takes you there. Heart disease takes you there. Chronic pain takes you there. Welcome!

I'm afraid there are monsters awaiting you in the cave. Here are some.
- Fear
- Humiliation and subjection
- Loneliness
- The loss of time

Fear

I do not know any way of describing the fear of death that can suddenly balloon up inside you, or the horrible blind terror that can come when you are bleeding uncontrollably or your heart rhythms are chaotic, or even, just in the night, when you feel Death standing by your bedside, poised with a wet scarf to hold against your face. Fear hangs round with Infirmity, awaiting its moment.

For me the best antidote is my Christian faith, or specifically my conviction that I am held in the arms of a loving God. '*We will not fear though the earth gives way and the mountains be moved into the heart of the sea.*'[5]

But I do also see the value of just hanging in there when the terror of death strikes, and the need to do some practical things first. The most practical thing is to seek the company of another human. Sorry if this is not very profound. Just telling someone else about the dark place you are in is a good start when you are overwhelmed by your own thoughts. Hopefully the person you approach will freak out less than you are freaking out and will offer practical suggestions. Then, endure. Endurance can be a good quality to develop, a treasure in the cave, and can be a good fruit that comes out of the terror of death or out of many trials. So you are being swept with fear. You have done the necessary things, with help. Good. So now your battle is with your mind, not your circumstances. Ask yourself: what, realistically, would you like to do again before death harvests you? And what would you like to put right? This takes your mind from dwelling on the panic and relocates it in the realms of hope and life.

---

[5] The English Standard Version (ESV) of Psalm 46:2.

My guess is that your answers will be located somewhere in the realm of belonging (to do with the people and communities we love) and making (our way of making the world a bit more lovely). Focus on those and fight the fear with them. Determine to do those things. Fight for the right to do them again. Sure you may be bleeding into the toilet or pain may be spreading through your chest, but fight the fear. It's going to cripple you if you don't. Fight for the reason and the right to go on living. Then, when the bleeding stops, the pain subsides, the heartbeat resumes, or the ambulance comes, you can store away those lessons for later use. And you can note that you've been on an endurance boot camp, and the experience will help you in the next crisis.

It's an expensive way to get an education! But since you've paid the fees, you may as well keep the notes. Those things you fought the fear with are discoveries that you can keep with you. What do you want to do before you die? What do you want to put right? What do you want to make good? Where will your joy come from? Focus on those.

Humiliation and subjection

The next worst thing about infirmity (that I can think of) is humiliation and subjection. Really, you thought slavery had been abolished but sudden infirmity ushers us back to the place of victimhood.

So much about lived-out infirmity is humiliation. You walk so slowly in the street that old people overtake you and others look away, trying not to stare. You carry your own urine, golden and glistening, in a polythene bag. You fall over in the street. I've done all of these and I've watched other people as they've done them too and I've marvelled at their calmness and fortitude. I just felt shame.

Or perhaps you are a hard worker, facing the shame of watching someone else clean your room or your dishes, or your bottom.

Infirmity restricts your liberty, another unwelcome surprise. My first experience of a ward, usually, is that they take away all my medicines and lock them in a cupboard. They do this to everyone so if we were to have a breakdown through excessive stress, we can't kill ourselves by eating all our pills. (Hospitals? Stressful? Surely not.) Then they take responsibility for putting my light on and off, for waking me in the morning at their convenience, for feeding me even if it isn't really time for a meal, and for dispensing my drugs. Having locked up my meds they quite often dispense the right drug at the right time, but not so often that I can take my guard down.

And more slavery and humiliation. With cannulas bandaged into both wrists, that I don't want to get wet, I've been given a bowl of water and told to wash and shave. I've lain naked in an operating theatre with people looking at my private parts and deciding if they can insert a tube in my groin despite a skin rash. I've been woken at four in the morning to have blood taken, having just got to sleep. I've lain in bed for an hour waiting for a strip light to be turned off, with none of us in the ward mobile enough to do it ourselves. I've been hoisted naked onto a toilet with a mechanical crane. Think about these things. In a few hundred years, history teachers will enjoy teaching children about 21st century medicine, doctors shoving metal into people and sawing and poisoning and irradiating them. Girls will faint in these classes. It will be

like our day when history teachers go long on Tudor
torture chambers. Kids then will not believe those things
were ever done. But they will have been done, to you and
me.

My first time in hospital, aged 8, I cried because I was
lonely and I couldn't eat the hospital food. Aged 51, in
hospital again, I cried for the same reasons, and also
because, like when I was 8, I'd been good for a long time
and didn't have anything left to be brave with anymore.

I have seen the stress of others. I have heard patients
become abusive and violent. I've watched people defecate
in bed and I've watched a pool of urine flow from my next-
door cubicle in Accident and Emergency into mine. If
you've never suffered infirmity, do hang around. All this
awaits you. Probably you'll be deaf as well by then and be
shouted at by a nurse whose English isn't great.

Being a carer of someone is almost as bad as if the
infirmity was your own: the pain of going into a room or
climbing onto a bus with the kind of person who needs a
full-time carer. It's not that people aren't kind, though
perhaps some are not. Almost, it is that they are kind, that
they need to be kind, that they find you and the person
you are with some object that needs to be treated with
kindness rather than simply treated as an ordinary human
being. You feel the shame of it all.

So much cave. Where are the jewels? For me they are
around the discovery of the small. Surviving enslavement
is about taking things a day at a time, a step at a time, a
meal at a time. A joy at a time if possible. It's not
particularly profound. It's merely learning the ability to
take the next step. Sufficient to the day is the evil thereof;

don't worry about tomorrow. Just do today. We only have today. Today is the space we all do all our living in. Endure today. Find a piece of sunlight today. Eat a pie today. Do the day and then tomorrow do tomorrow. This, again, is a good find to keep in your pocket all your life. You can't stockpile future happiness, so find today's.

One day you'll be released from hospital. Carry this lesson with you and you'll be like one of the rocks on the coastline, not fearing the future seasons, and even when battered by wave after wave, still standing, sometimes catching the sunlight.

Loneliness

There's a loneliness to being sick or infirm. There's also a great loneliness, a separate loneliness, to being a carer. What is it to be lonely? I think it is to be isolated from the herd. This is a hard part of the cave. We humans have a natural distaste for the sick or the irregular. If you happen to be sick or irregular, or the carer of one, you feel the shunning of the herd. What treasures can we unearth in this dark part of the cave? I can think of two:

The fellowship of the suffering
The discipline of hope.

Meet with others who have also been rendered lonely by loss or infirmity. Meet them somehow. Those who have suffered are members of an exclusive club and only those who have paid the large entrance fee are allowed in.

It really is a remarkable club. Every member of the club has things they can give to every other member, and every member has things they can receive from every other member. The members know and strengthen each other. You don't need a special handshake to recognize each other, merely a shared experience of adversity.

The cave has plenty of deeper caverns to which I have not paid the entrance fees. But even in my beginners' part of the cave, I can find strength, and I can know people and belong. Shunned by a world that has evolved to shun infirmity, I find I have been given a membership pass to deep connection. When you've suffered loss or infirmity you've learnt a special language than only others who have suffered can understand, but in your communication you find all the things we normally get from being a normal part of the human herd: healing and laughter and tears and sympathy and strength.

The other way to combat the loneliness of loss and adversity is the discipline of hope. It is raising your eyes to the wider horizon. It is based in the will and is somewhat systematic. It is asking and answering the question, 'What will I do again that will make this bleak present worth enduring?' The answer is not what you'd wish to do, but what you intend to do. Again I would not be surprised if your hope was located somewhere in the area of belonging or building or beautifying. Hope of contributing again is a ticket to wholeness and also a ticket to being accepted back into the herd.

I remember one of the times I fell over in the street, just outside my home. My face had hit concrete, an experience I have yet to really enjoy. I was alone and the street was quiet. The only thing was to wait there a bit and then get up. I remembered while I lay there thinking about a new car. I received generous disabled benefits that enabled me to lease a new car every three years, paid for by the taxpayer. Sometimes you could add your own money to upgrade to a model of your choice. My wife and I had been thinking about the next one, and she had separately mentioned that she admired someone's convertible Mini. On the paving slab that day I decided we would lease a convertible Mini, in British Racing Green, and Cordelia and I would buzz around in it together and do stuff. Whether or not my legs kept buckling, she and I could rejoin the human herd again, joyously, in our British Racing Green convertible Mini.

As it turned out, we eventually found that car didn't quite suit us, and we got something else instead. But the central hope came true. I got to spend more years with Cordelia, and we still buzzed around and did stuff. I don't altogether know where the thought of a new car came from, when I was lying on the paving stones, but I do know it was a much better thought than the equally plausible thoughts *this is a nightmare* or *I'm never going to be right again*. I also know that that spark of hope somehow fired an engine that helped me to get up; the hope itself, which was plausible and attainable, had power to do me good. So, hope for a better day. Or if that's too much, at least hope for a good moment or two, sometime in the future.

The waste of time

Still another surprise about infirmity or adversity is how much time you are wasting. You might be too sick to do whatever it is you used to do. You might also be spending hours shuttling between medical appointments. The people around you are busy and carrying extra loads, and if you look at them carefully you can see the lines of tiredness and worry on their faces.

You may rage against this. The fruitful thing, the thing you were good at, the thing that was a real contribution, that thing, you can't do any more. Worse, no-one else is doing it, or they are not doing it that well. Still worse, perhaps time is passing away and it will never get done, and it was important. How can we make sense of this?

It's hard not to sound flip. But everything in our world has seasons: day and night, sleep and activity, winter and spring and summer. The winters and nights are frustrating but they are also times of stripping back to the essentials. Over some months when I was convalescing, my wife put all my emails into a folder called 'trashed by Cordelia.' Sometimes I think she wrote to people explaining I was too ill to reply. Nothing bad happened, the world continued to spin, and indeed when I started emails again I realized how life-sapping many of them were.

Maybe your busy life before your infirmity wasn't all that fruitful. Perhaps you were working or entertaining yourself to death. Perhaps those former busy days were the real waste of your time, heaping up a mound of empty achievements.

The habits you can learn crossing the deserts of wasted time are disciplines for all of life that you can take with you. The main lesson? You are not invaluable. When you are forced to stop, you hear the crashing as all the plates you were spinning hit the floor. But then the world carries on. As if you didn't matter. Maybe you *don't* matter. Actually you probably *do* matter, a lot, but not in the ways you think. Stopping helps us work these things out. What's happening? What was once important is less important and what was once unimportant or you were too busy for is suddenly discovered as important. You've been wrong all these years about your priorities. Through the seasoning of wasted time you can find new and better reasons to live.

What being seasoned looks like

So: our exploration of infirmity unearths some more valuable lessons of adversity, some more aspects of seasoning— our treasures in the cave. Here's a summary:

1. *Sharing our darkness with others*. Like hidden wiring, being honest about our pain with another person can plug us into energy and strength.

2. *Enduring*. This is just hanging in there; recognizing that your current hardship *is* hardship, and very unpleasant, but deciding to ride it out anyway.

3. *Recognizing seasons*. Closely related to endurance, this is giving you a bit of perspective that your miserable *now* is not an *always*; and that the practices you develop in your miserable nows will sustain you in the alwayses.

4. *Being determined to find joy*. It might be small, you might have to hunt around, but joy is a gift for the now. Joyful people are those who develop a lifetime habit of stringing together lots of these joyful nows. Joyful people lift the spirits of the people they meet.

5. *Doing hope*. As we have seen, hope is not just vaguely wishing things would improve, but being determined to do some achievable, life-giving thing again.

Adversity or loss or infirmity or disappointment or something has brought us to a crunching halt. We are looking out at a landscape with a sobriety and clarity that is aided by our low mood. We are beginning to realize that there is quite a lot that is more important behind the glitzy and temporary frontage to a life of success, wealth or popularity. These are helpful thoughts, sobering. What do we do now? What parts of our mental landscape do we stop visiting? What new paths do we tread down?

The broken dream, and the good questions

I want to suggest that the main place not to visit is the *broken dream*.

I would have liked to have splashed along the seashore one day, with one of my children on my shoulder. I never have—I never could—and now I never will. It would be maudlin and stupid to think on this, a small thing. You may have proper things to mourn. I'm not saying you should never visit a broken dream. But really. Clear up, say your goodbyes, tie everything off. Let it go back to nature. It's always going to be part of you, but it is a better part of you when it shapes a new future, rather than when it is a decaying present you are trying to primp, or when you are using it to define who you are today. You need to define yourself by something other than your loss, your sorrow, your ill-health, your former hopes, or your former state.

Instead of mooching around your broken dream, enjoying the gothic scene of heartbreak, your loosened hair romantically draped over the headstone of your loss, you might want to ask a few questions now that the urgency of your loss has passed. This is the path to healing. Don't feel the need to answer these hurriedly. Mull them over. Work them into your life.

What have I not lost?
What do I love?
Whom do I love?
What do I value?

Point your feet where these answers direct you. Keep asking the questions and keep walking in the answers. You won't fix everything in an afternoon, or a year, or in the rest of your life, but you will be walking the right road and you will at times find yourself in the green pastures and quiet waters that you have always wanted. Instead of a darkening autumn or a barren winter, I do believe you may smell the spring.

The discovery of the everyday

So, seeking what really matters matters. So does thankfulness, and thankfulness for the ordinary.

Contentment, someone said, is desiring what you already have. As we recover from experiences of failure or infirmity, usually by treading down new pathways in our heads, we have a class in learning about what we already have and what of that is worth keeping.

A friend of mine whose wife was dying wrote how much he and she just enjoyed being together. Their upcoming parting reminded them of the value of a shared meal or conversation or even just watching TV together. It was quotidian stuff, everyday pleasures, but they found it at the core of what made life good:

Enjoy life with your wife, whom you love, all the days of this meaningless life that God has given you under the sun—all your meaningless days. [6]

Remember the failure pyramid a few sections back? The one with a few superstars at the top and the aspiring, unsuccessful masses at the base? Wrong model. The world is more like a range of hills and lakes, crossed with hiking paths. It doesn't matter that you don't climb to the top of the highest peak. There are thousands of other routes, bracing, glorious routes, with which you will happily fill a hiking life. Once you shake yourself free of the untruth that *I must get to the top*—and a few years in a seasoning shed helps with that—you are free to enjoy the hiking paths all your days. On these paths, you do whatever it is you do, alongside thousands of others who are also doing whatever it is they do. And none of you are at the top. Ordinary? Yes. Good? Yes. Happy? If you let suffering teach you humility, yes.

When I was a student, my friends and I pushed against the ordinariness from which we had come. We wanted to make a splash. We wanted to live radical lives and change the world. 'We want to run a totally open home,' one said, everyone welcome, everyone fed, anyone can stay the night. I remember one of my friends saying she didn't want ever to have a mortgage. She wanted to rent all her life so that she was flexible and free, not tied down and conventional.

My friends are living striking and distinctive lives, but I have observed that they, like me, also came to embrace the ordinary. When it is focused on spending time with

---

[6] The Book of Ecclesiastes 9:9

people you love, work you love, locations you love, day after day, ordinary life can be very good. It is wealth. It is treasure. When you are denied it, you learn the deep loss from not having it. Both the working for and the attaining of the ordinary brings meaning and contentment into our lives.

Wealth and success can rob you of ordinariness, which is quite a surprise since wealth and success are supposed to bring happiness. But just as there are burglars who are greatly relieved to be caught, so there are successful people who are greatly relieved to pass out of the limelight. In both cases, a weight is lifted.

Friendship

We are wrapped in a web of relationships. Sometimes our relational threads stretch to surprising people. The love embedded here is not always expressed, but adversity brings it to the surface. Their love for you is suddenly exposed in cards, notes, visits, gifts, calls, prayers. And you respond. Adversity gets you and them to say things that you've always meant to say. Saying them is a great gift and blessing. Letting love and pride flow back and forth down these threads of love, sprinkling them with tears probably, is not just a help to healing and thriving. It is itself the primary act of healing and thriving. Further repairs to your body or circumstances that may or may not follow are secondary. If you are lucky enough to be surrounded by a web of love, and most of us are, adversity is the time to know this and invest in it.

What a treasure this is. In May 2011, in Palo Alto, California, a girl was sitting at the kitchen table doing her homework when there was a knock on the kitchen door.

36

She went to open it and found Bill Gates standing outside. Upstairs the girl's father, Steve Jobs, was ill with the cancer that would end his life. The girl let Gates in, and Gates and Jobs, the two rival tech titans, engineer and zen-gineer, spent time together. They talked, it is reported, about families and children and marrying well, and about Jobs' plans for his yacht.[7] Gates' visit, it seems, was to maintain, perhaps to fix, but in any case to re-emphasize, a relational thread between the founder of Microsoft and the founder of Apple.

A friend of mine who was dying of cancer pointed out that one of the good things about her cancer was that she got time to say goodbye. Among other things, my friend arranged a party for all the women she trained with decades before. I observed her cancer was not a stressy round of treatments, anger, bitterness and disappointment but a kind of packing and farewelling for the next journey.

I agree that some adversity is better than other sorts for spurring relational goodness. In some adversity (illness, say), people send love and cards and you will feel their support; in other forms (a bad marriage, or bad breath, say), even your closest friends will fear to intrude and the shops tend not to stock cards.

But whether or not your adversity is the sort of adversity for which people send cards (*Congratulations on 25 years of Irritable Bowels!*), I still think any adversity can be manhandled into making you unearth good in yourself

---

[7] The meeting is reported in Walter Isaacson's biography of Steve Jobs and it was previewed by Forbes magazine: https://www.forbes.com/sites/briancaulfield/2011/10/20/bill-gates-and-steve-jobs-their-final-meeting/#5601d04e512c

and those around you. So your anxiety or your IBS goes on and on? So does your resolve.

Set things right. Heal the relationships. Fix these things that you can fix and your whole world will be brighter. Setting things right means:

- Saying the unsaid
- Mending the broken
- Straightening the bent
- Tying up the loose ends

Here are some suggestions for improving your friendship connection with your fellow humans, with eternity, and with yourself:

- Say everything good that needs saying to your loved ones. Don't wait to regret not saying these things when you die.
- Make peace with your enemies.
- Get your affairs in order.
- Work on your eulogy virtues, the things they will say at your funeral, like that you were kind, rather than your resume (CV) virtues such as your salesperson-of-the-year-runner's-up award.
- Sort out the God-and-eternity business in your soul.
- Gratefully relish each 'bright blessed day', and 'dark sacred night'.

The joy of walking pace

Embrace the slow. This is linked with other habits that adversity causes us to respect, such as taking a day at a time and taking pleasure in small things. The person who embraces slow doesn't dream of some day when everything will be wonderful, when they win the lottery or retire. Those who embrace slow point their feet in the direction of their dreams and start taking a few steps. It doesn't matter that the road is hundreds of miles long. Just being on the road is itself contentment and fulfilment and it is the beginnings of fruitfulness and usefulness.

Some things are slow by their nature, for example helping small human beings become big ones. Many other things, like wealth or friendship, thrive under the same treatment. You keep doing the small, good, prudent, wise things and watch the power of compound interest. What you sow you reap, which is extraordinary when what you sow is small, and insignificant, and done in wintry fields, and what you reap is great, lovely and a thing of high summer. All that bridges the gap between seed and harvest is your patient repetition and the passage of time. If time is an enemy of the faithless, it is a good friend of the faithful. You can cover miles and miles at walking pace.

All is not lost when all is lost

Here's another path to tread in your head: do small things well even if big things have collapsed around you. Your great loss may not be as total as it seems; and your small acts of goodness add up. Roiled around by the mighty tides of time, the little good things can overwhelm the big bad thing.

We can demonstrate this at both smaller and larger scales. Imagine you made a mistake at work. Imagine the mistake was not just human error but due to carelessness, ill-temper or even malice. Then imagine two separate responses:

- Cover up, minimize, self-justify
- Apologize, admit your fault, ask forgiveness.

Which is the better 'strategy'? Much more important, which has integrity? Which behaviour will, in the end, do you the most good? Which path leads to the least complicated life? And which path, over time, will get you the respect you seek, and we all need?

Think of defeat and victory on a larger scale. Think of Nelson Mandela. He was troublesome and didn't renounce violence. The South African state locked him up for life, with hard labour, a victory for them and a setback for him. He was off the streets and mostly out of the newspapers.

Mandela spent his 50th birthday in jail. Then his 60th. And then his 70th. But it turns out that maintaining injustice in a society is like trying to hold a beach ball under water. While Mandela passed milestone birthdays, the South African state was exhausting itself. Internally, it was fighting to maintain injustice, against protests of every kind. Externally, it was facing a crisis of belonging: its membership of the club of civilised countries was being stressed by the general issue of national racism and the specific dunked beachball called Mandela. The real, jailed Mandela, working the limestone quarry on Robben Island, took every rare opportunity to study and lobby and organize.

Eventually time's pressure on the state grew too much and the state folded. In his seventies, Mandela walked out of prison and into the presidency. The little good things he'd spent twenty years doing overwhelmed the big bad thing done to him. As president, he worked to reconcile the nation and he left when his time was up rather than clinging to office. In the contest, Mandela *v* South Africa, who won and who lost? How did the winner win and how did the loser lose? What part did time play? How did repeated small acts of integrity fare against large doses of injustice?

Think of an even larger scale. Strip the story of Jesus of Nazareth down to its politics: popular leader gets into the faces of the politico-religious elite and shows their falseness. They arrest him. He doesn't defend himself. They execute him while he prays for their forgiveness. And then they lose control of history. Time compounds this, a rumour of resurrection fuels it, and now a third of humanity notionally walks under the banner of 'Christian'. As projects go, stamping out Christianity can't be deemed a success.

I guess you can think of counter examples. But the gains of slow faithfulness are impressive. How can your honest apology at work enhance your reputation? How can a jailbird destroy apartheid? How can your adversity-limited life be productive and good? Small steps.

A summary

Let's collect up and summarize the lessons of adversity:

We are ordinary.

We are poor.

We are broken.

There will be losses.

Time compounds things, so it's a good idea to live with integrity in both the large and the small. Integrity will still be holding your hand when charisma, success, pride and boasting, and your good looks, even yours, are mottled and crinkled.

Approaching problems and joys a day at a time, or a moment at a time, means you tackle them at a scale you were built for and can manage.

Our life in the midst of others—belonging to others, making peace with others, exposing our lusts and terrors and darkness to the kind light of others—is key to walking the long distance of life well. Suffering shared can lead to deep connection which is life.

Hoping and resolving to do something right and good, or to live towards the doing of something good, is a mighty weapon in the fight to reclaim your mind from itself. Even if it's slow. Even if it feels like small steps upward after a catastrophic fall. Why? You find you are working with the grain of the Universe. The Danish philosopher and theologian Søren Kierkegaard wrote a book with the title *Purity of Heart is to Will One Thing*. What a magnificent insight. (Perhaps I should read the book.) There is a course of life for us that is fruitful, being what we are, doing what we do, some good thing. It might be quite ordinary. Progress may be slow. Seasons may change while we await its fulness. But it is the path of life.

BELONGING

The story so far: adversity burns off much that is false about our lives and helps us focus on the important strands. I count two: belonging and making. This chapter is about belonging.

Spending your days investing in your bonds with family and other networks of belonging might seem the biggest waste of time, for example when you fidget through a committee meeting or hear a dribbly grandad tell you the same story for the twenty-third time, or when you are using up your childbearing years caring for a needy relative.

Ask yourself: how did our human species become as successful as the brown rat or the cockroach? We don't have fur or armour. We break, bruise and burn. Little antelopes and zebras can be galloping across the savannah within hours; little humans still fall over a lot after eighteen months, not good for escaping big cats or even little ones. So how did we succeed? Partly because we were individually smart and flexible. And mostly because we have learnt the power of belonging, the superhuman power of being a cluster of people who work together. We've leveraged belonging into a world-spanning, globe-conquering superpower.

A mammoth can feed a village but think of the problem of hunting one. Especially if it's just you, unarmed, against a thick-skinned, long-tusked pachyderm with a yen for continuing to exist. The odds change when the contest is between a mammoth and a cooperating group of humans. They can surround the mammoth and scare it so that it panics and runs off a cliff. Butcher it with flint knives and everyone can eat their fill. A group of unarmed humans, with a large supply of nearby mammoths, could do that every week, like a weekly shopping trip. With this regular supply of protein, they would be free to build villages and raise families and create culture. Why are there no mammoths left in the world? In their five-million-year span on earth they survived a lot of threats, like climate change. There were still mammoths on a remote Russian island when the pyramids were being built. But they were the last of the noble line; and organized humans, hunting in packs, arguably came for them too.

Cooperation is our superpower. With it, we feed the world, build safe homes, cure diseases, lengthen life and successfully store and pass on the expertise so that 30,000 days later, a whole new planetful of humans can stand on our shoulders and see further and achieve more. Over a few thousand years, our superpower has made us such a force that, though we are just a single species, we are shaping earth, sea and the skies (though not necessarily in good ways). Fractious and quarrelsome as we may be, warlike and tribal, nevertheless, we are extraordinary—together.

Crowds vs. networks

'Belonging' is one way of saying 'being part of a network'. A network, as I mean it here, is a group of people linked by relationships.

Not all collections of people are networks. Here's what aren't networks: queues, crowds, traffic jams, flocks of tourists. Here are some examples of what are, or can become networks: a sports team, a squad of soldiers, an orchestra, a village fete, a live event when performers and crowd are feeding off each other, a classroom, a family. All these can become sustaining communities that people love and fight for.

What's the difference between a crowd and a network? Human relationships. Crowds that aren't networks are life-draining; networks of people, working together, are life-sustaining. I have been in traffic jams so profound that they turn into networks because drivers leave their vehicles and start talking with each other. A sports team can be transformed once it stops being a crowd of stars—or a crowd of mediocrities—and works as a networked, relational whole.

Networks let us pool and share our talents. They provide resources, guidance and self-worth. They protect us from external foes and, by setting norms, they save us from ourselves. And they satisfy our deep needs to belong and contribute.

During the past couple of decades in the UK I have watched pubs close and coffee-shops open. The way we network is changing; the need to network isn't, and making networking happen will always be good business.[8]

Networks and life-support

As well as being our superpower, networks are our source of meaning and life.

I have two scrapbooks in my study from my coma-month. One was created by my family, one by the Intensive Care staff. They document what was going on with me in ICU, and in the world outside. My family have stuck in some of the cards and emails they received while I was ill. They also pasted news reports I might have liked. And they added in the letters they wrote to me. I cannot read these books (or, it turns out, write about them) without the tears flowing.

They are so extraordinarily moving, almost intolerable, these scrapbooks. While I lay on my back plugged into medical machinery, a middle-aged, red-faced white man, the sort that you wouldn't look twice at, heart disease fodder, my loved ones laboured under a burden of care and fear and fought my death like tigers. They read my books to me, they talked to me, they read Terry Pratchett novels. A doctor saw my mum mopping my brow and asked her why she was doing that. 'He's burning up,' she told him. The doctor turned, walked away, visited the other ICU ward, and came back with an ice-blanket, the only one in the hospital, and got me wrapped in it.

---

[8] I'm indebted to Nicholas A Christakis and James H Fowler's *Connected* (New York: Little, Brown 2009) for their insights. Theirs is the best book on networking that I've ever seen.

Each day, the ICU staff tenderly washed and shaved me.

Normally we moderate our expressions of love. Normally our loving hearts beat for each other under a coating of banter, criticism and everyday chat. Sometimes the coating is so thick we wonder if a heart beats under there at all. Death or near-death or the threat of death strips the coating away and we briefly feel the raging incandescence of human love. I think it is the greatest thing in the world. My coma-books are like me enjoying my own funeral without having to die: everybody's kind to me and they don't mention my faults. Their love also repaints my insides with sunshine.

A couple of weeks after I left ICU, but before I was finally discharged from hospital, my wife wheeled me round to the unit again. She was hoping to fill in some of the gaps in my memory. I was surprised to find that the nurses seemed to know me; I didn't know any of them. My wife pointed things out. *That* was the room where the doctor told her that I wasn't expected to survive the night. *That* nurse was the one assigned to me when I was hallucinating that it was our daughter's wedding day, and I was trying to get out of bed, and almost weeping with frustration that I couldn't. (I remembered that day. The nurse had told me that they would put a phone near my ear so that I could hear the service. Then, presumably after talking to my family, she reassured me it wasn't my daughter's wedding day at all, that was still weeks away, and I remember the surge of relief and the joy of allowing myself to fall back to sleep.)

I told this nurse from my wheelchair how sorry I was for causing all that nuisance, and I thought later how she was one of those people in the hospital who transcends treating you as a nurse only and treats you as a fellow human sufferer too. She wasn't paid to care as much as she did care, and what a thing it is to find (as I often did in hospital) medical staff journeying well beyond professional expertise into deep humanity, caring for me.

It is overwhelming how important networks are to us. I don't know how often you ask questions like, *What have I achieved? What was the point? What am I proud of?* Or even *Why do I bother continuing to live?* For me, the answer to all of that is being part of a network of people who apparently love me as much as I love them. Nothing else compares. I've been a writer all my life but in all the millions of words I've sprayed about the place, happy though that has been, that career has not offered a quality of meaning or healing or worth to compare with the simple discovery of being loved by my loved ones. The loving network trumps everything.

Let me add to my point by looking at this from the other end.

Probably we can all think of someone who died for no good reason except that they became separate from the network that had sustained them. Maybe they retired, maybe their spouse died, maybe they relocated. Maybe just nobody ever liked them very much and what friends they had fell away. Their death certificate won't have recorded the real cause, disconnection and loneliness.

I worked a bit for some years among young people involved in crime. Everyone knows these youths share a lot in common, for example: low educational achievement, poverty, broken homes, ADHD. But now I think about it, isolation, unwantedness, not belonging, is central to these kids' experience. Nobody loves them. Some were chucked out of their mum's home at age 16, no longer welcome. Others have lost the last stable person in their life, a grandad say, and fallen into a hole. The sustaining network in which they should have grown up has betrayed them. These youngsters still form networks, but they tend not to be healthy networks.

Separately I also work a little among my fellow-disabled people. (Interestingly, many of these people are the same people who used to be involved in youth crime, just older now; this is a pointer to the long shadow that broken childhood networks can cast.) In my work among the disabled I once came across a woman who lived alone, isolated by her many infirmities, and who suffered anxiety and depression. The only reason she hadn't killed herself, she reported, was because she didn't want to upset her cats. This unfortunate woman's network was her cats.

The family

Our families are our smallest and closest network and that is so obvious little needs to be said. When the hijacked plane over Pennsylvania on 9/11 got phone signal, who were the calls between? When the chaplain talks with the dying on a battlefield, to whom do they send messages? In the covid-19 pandemic in the UK, visitors were not allowed in hospital; nurses lent out their own mobile phones so dying patients could say goodbye to their families. We know instinctively that family is the first network of welfare and care. The poet Robert Frost famously wrote, 'Home is the place where, when you have to go there, they have to let you in.' One of the psalms describes God as one who 'sets the lonely in families'.[9] Functional families are an astonishing good.

Social networks

Wider networks also support and shape us. One of the main reasons for the 20th century fashion of studying for an MBA was the network of contacts it provided. Around the world, young people scrabble (or parents scrabble on their behalf) to enter schools or universities as much for the networks as for the education or the personal formation. If you want a job offer, or a manuscript published, or to make a sale, or to run a country, join the right network. If you want to be president of the US, history teaches us, you must belong to either the Republican or Democrat network. At the time of writing, no independent individual, however blessed with political superpowers, has achieved what these networks achieve every few years, getting someone the most powerful job in the world.

Gangs are networks; churches and denominations are networks. The best way of finding almost anything, plumber, piano teacher or spouse, has traditionally been the network of your friends' friends. (The internet may be disrupting all this but it is reconfiguring human networks, not substituting for them.) Authors, agents, editors, reps and booksellers used to make up the bookselling network, and to sell a book you had to join that network. That's changing too, but it's being supplanted by new networks not no networks.

---

[9] Psalm 68:6, NIVUK

How can a mentally ill or very needy person be cared for in a community? Any solo human would probably be sucked dry by the person's neediness. But a suitable network can ensure that person takes their meds, has someone to go to for a cup of coffee, has someone to call round and check they've washed recently, and has friends whom they can call on the phone. No-one gets burnt or carries too much. The network can sustain a quality of life for someone that would exhaust the solo carer.

The creation network

One more network still. We live interdependently with the Universe and especially the planet Earth.

Evolution teaches us that nearly all our best bits – eyes, wombs, fingers – were developed and road-tested by other creatures in an earlier age. Like all current life on earth, we are a plundered scrapyard of earlier forms. Perhaps the best bits of our brains are the only bits other creatures have never had. Without a vast network of life, stretching back through time, you wouldn't exist or have all the wonderful body parts you have. The network of life made you, as much as God did.

As we learnt at school, when we breathe out, plants breathe in. All the chemical companies in the world can't match this ancient, intricate network for oxygen production. We can't make our own drinking water either: we mostly just siphon off the water that the planetary network delivers via the water cycle. We can't fuel or maintain our bodies without feasting on an unthinkable network of creatures who themselves either eat other creatures or who have mastered exotic skills like turning sunlight into sugar and protein. The reason spaceflight is so hard is because we are trying to maintain human life outside the normal sustaining network of the life of Planet Earth.

Unsurprisingly, exposure to this network is itself life-giving. Among the good things that many of us have taken away from the Covid-19 pandemic is a fresh enjoyment of the creation network, and how it restores life.

You will see straight away there are complexities here. The virus that caused Covid-19 and killed all its millions was itself a product of the creation network, just another young virus innocently making its way in the world. 'Mother Nature' is not entirely to be trusted. She is rather reckless in the matter of scorpions, slugs, boils, and mass-extinctions. If you grow vegetables on a shared plot in Cambridge, as we do, you soon learn that bringing a crop to harvest is like some Cold-War-era battle with the Russians. You are attacked from every direction, from underground, from the surface, and biologically, and from the air. Even when you successfully defend your plants from snails, blight, butterflies and birds, crack squads of urban-hardened micro deer, called muntjacs, conduct daring night-time raids. They leap tall fences in a single bound, wriggle through small gaps, and feast on your sweetcorn in the moonlight. Creation, for all its wonderfulness, is a network that requires plenty of human intervention for humans to thrive in. It is refreshing and life-giving, but merely 'going back to nature,' whatever that means, would be a public health disaster. Some people think humans are a parasite or a pestilence in the creation network; on the contrary, however well or badly we are doing, ours are the only voices on the planet of compassion and good sense. [10]

The use and abuse of networks

Our relation to the creation network is emblematic of a larger truth. Networks both nurture and harm. People can seize control of networks and milk them to their satisfaction and our loss. This means 'belonging' is an active verb, not a passive one.

An example: Dictators are network-plunderers on a national scale. Why do they like military parades? Why do they fill stadiums with synchronized dancing schoolgirls? Why do they put posters of themselves everywhere? Why do they so hate criticism and put comedians in jail? These are the network-deprived, draping themselves with networks, but never satisfying the hunger inside.

The same is true on a smaller scale. Unhealthy networks, even ones where love is present, can also injure us. A job you love can be turned into a job you hate by a misfiring workplace network.

Network abuse within families or other realms of love and trust is among the most effective ways of cruelly damaging a human being. The natural currents of love that should circulate within families can be joined by

---

[10] This does not mean I am not a fan of the 'rewilding' movement. I am. But I think rewilding parts of the land and ocean is itself best envisaged as part of a wider scheme for the thriving of humans and Creation, which may require both rewilded and more traditionally farmed areas, all under human care.

unnatural currents of abuse in a dysfunctional family network. This is crushing. Why do so few women leave abusive or coercive partners? Why do they take so long when they do? Of the 700 murders that take place in the UK each year, around 100 are women killed by their intimate partners, each one choosing to live on in a household of control and increasing violence that is obvious to an outsider. Why don't they leave? Because the joint impact of love and toxicity, the nurturing and the brutality, the way that the natural place of support and health has also become the unnatural place of injury and death, that dilemma, has turned their brains to smashed avocados. It's hard to leave an abusive network because it's always hard to leave a network because even an abusive network provides stuff we need. No wonder common sense disintegrates.

Fruitfulness and our networks

How do we ensure healthy human networks? We can't necessarily. But most of us learn some of the arts. I want to underline two of them: subordination and subversion.

Subordination is an unfashionable word. It means fitting in with the greater whole. Marriages and relationships work with a degree of subordination to each other. In the workplace most of us understand the need to work, co-operate, fit in, serve—to subordinate ourselves. In this way we feed the network, and as time compounds our efforts, eventually the network feeds us. Politicians seeking votes see the need to subordinate themselves to party activists and even as a last resort, to the actual electorate. Here in the UK, each member of parliament is elected by a local area, and most politicians learn the value of knocking on doors and meeting the voters, slowly, one by one. The primary system in the US pitches presidential candidates into ordinary living rooms to sell their wares.

Yet we also need a rebelliousness in our networking, holding it loosely, ready to slip away, unafraid to change or to drive the network to change.

Next time you meet a witch being burnt at the stake, ask her what she thinks of grassroots movements. Networks can be bad or grow bad or become irrelevant in a changing world. As networked beings we need to learn how to change them. This is hard. We need to combine loyalty with critique, indulging a capacity for satire or subversion. Psychologists sometimes talk about our need for autonomy. We need to learn the art of staying true to what we know to be good, and if necessary subverting the status quo.

Networks are sticky. That is, they organize humans in such a way that they can become hard to change, and that inflexibility can cause the network to become irrelevant or even evil: nasty civil wars and deadly feuds erupt and persist through generations when one community stickily crashes against another. So we who belong to networks need to belong loyally, but also critically.

The best example of loyal subversion I know is the Jewish prophet Jeremiah. He lived in Israel four centuries back into the Old Testament when the Jewish nation was a rump state based around Jerusalem. It was widely believed in Jeremiah's network that Jerusalem was impregnable because it was well-fortified and because the

Temple was there, and God would look after it as he had for hundreds of years. A whirring hamster-wheel of religious ritual, singing Psalms and singeing dead sheep, constituted regular payments of this insurance premium. The religio-political network had grown sticky and rigid in its long years of operation.

Jeremiah watched the rise of the Babylonian empire, a regional superpower. He perceived prophetically that the Babylonians were going to invade and destroy Israel, and that this was a judgement from God.

The many pages of his prophetic writings are the story of his psychic agony as his loyalty to his network clashed with his desire to subvert it in God's name. He belonged to the network, but not so much that he was unable to call out the evil within. This did not make him a popular figure. Important people didn't believe him or like him. He was jailed for a time, flogged, and thrown once into a pit. He was falsely accused of deserting. When Jerusalem did indeed burn, the Babylonians rescued him from prison and would have treated him well. Jeremiah, however, decided not to switch networks. He stayed with the people who had already so abused him, even though, as he suspected, they would continue to not listen. Eventually, this remnant of Jewish survivors fled south to Egypt, taking Jeremiah along with them, still kicking off.

Jeremiah is a perfect example of someone who is loyal to their network but more deeply loyal to something, or someone, higher. Few of us manage this well. Yet the healthiest networks are the ones filled with independent-minded people. These people have the capacity for subordination, but also the capacity to rebel. Networks need a loyal opposition. They need satire and individuality and humanity. They work best when their members are true to the network but also true to everything their best selves know to be wise and humane. The reason this is true is that networks magnify our human capacities. So, depending on their members, networks can magnify greed, insecurity, ambition, corruption or abuse. Or they can be salted with goodness and altruism.

However big the network is, and however small we are, we can change networks. It might involve skills we've already discussed in this book: doing small good things often enough and well enough. And it might take time. The German student dissident Sophie Scholl took on the murderous might of Nazi Germany, armed with little more than a few student friends and a lot of leaflets. She was beheaded. Yet now the fascists are gone and they name streets after Sophie Scholl in a Germany that has spent the last several generations working for peace and not war.

Even Jeremiah's network, the Jewish nation, took to preserving Jeremiah's writings rather than burning them, long after he died. It is a feature of networks that one generation persecutes the disrupters while the next puts flowers on their graves. Helpfully, however, we don't have to die before the networks around us change: our little weapons of peace and goodness, repeated often, reinforced by time, can make the difference even while we are still around to enjoy it.

So, yes, a good use of your time is the necessary suborning of yourself to those with whom you share the planet and with whom you share relationships. Another good use of your time is evaluating your relationship with your networks, because both they and you change, and because you have individual responsibility as a network member for what it is and does. Healthy networks are as vital as clean water or good food.

And yes, even though we only have about 30,000 days to spend in our one lifetime, it might mean the family party is important, or the lunch hour spent choosing and sending a card, or sitting on a committee for a season, or working on your organization's safeguarding policy. You can't do without a network, you have to learn the art of making them healthy. Belonging, being part of things, being networked, is the stuff of life: a privilege, a gift, a joy and a sorrow, a necessity, a duty and a dance.

MAKING

So:

We normally go through life following an ill-thought-out plan, chasing badly defined goals, hoping for the best, unlikely to find it.

Adversity can cause us to pivot, burning off some of our false expectations and focusing on useful ones.

One useful pivot is toward the discipline of belonging. This is a difficult art, needing frequent readjustment, but it is the stuff of life and an absolutely core act. Our networks protect us, sustain us, guide us and are a vehicle for service and self-worth. We must invest in them, while remaining autonomous within them. That way we create healthy networks and remain healthy people.

This chapter is about the second main direction to head: the making life.

What is the point of your life? Where are you heading? What is your purpose? What are you for?

A mark of depressed and isolated people is that they do not have an answer to these questions. A sign of your good mental health is that you do.

This purpose doesn't have to be a great thing. It can be a small thing, or a set of small things, but done with such attention and faithfulness that it becomes a great thing. Is it a small thing to manage to send a small child off to school, broadly on time, with lunch packed and sports kit washed? Is it a small thing to do your routine job for years, each day trying to do it a little better? These small things compound over time into huge things, a beautiful new adult launched into the world for example; or home, respect, security, friendships, peace and rest. You might start out as a little nut but with time and faithfulness you will become a great tree. According to Leo Tolstoy, General Kutuzov, who turned back Napoleon's great army in 1812, had a motto: 'time and patience.'

Let's further define making as 'making or doing a good thing', which loosens the link between working and earning, and which means that even if you are unemployed, disabled or retired, you can still, like a young chicken, run and find shelter under the great hen called 'making'.

Making on this definition is anything where you spend yourself doing something that increases the human-produced stock of good things in the universe. Making a rhubarb crumble counts. Going to a lecture, one of my favourite hobbies, counts, because you are learning and thinking. Running a nuclear power station counts. Arranging flowers or tidying your garden counts. Cleaning house counts. Fixing up your home counts. Caring for your spouse counts. Getting your home ready for a visit from your grandchildren counts. Serving others so that they are, or become, happy and fruitful counts.

I am not a fan of throwing stones at other religions beyond my own but I am certainly no fan either of religious or cultural systems that link what they consider 'dirty work' with 'dirty people'. *All* work, burying the dead with decency or cleaning a fatberg from a sewer system, is God's work. (Even if you don't believe in God you might be kind enough to consider what a God worthy of the role might do, patiently repairing the broken and forming the good.) In the street where I live are people who work for builders' merchants, people who teach other people how to use fire extinguishers, people who sell organic and fairly traded food, and people who design the computer chips that live in your mobile phone. Not to mention that all of us mow our lawns, buy our shopping and most of us clean our own toilets. It's all good.

I would go even further and say that making done in love, good work, is an unexpected and counterintuitive route to happiness, despite the fact we need to set alarms most days to stir us into it. The Jewish wisdom writers, editing their thoughts in the light of a charred homeland, dead friends, and the refugee experience, understood:

> *A person can do nothing better than to eat and drink and find satisfaction in their own toil. This too, I see, is from the hand of God, for without him, who can eat or find enjoyment?* [11]

> *I know that there is nothing better for people than to be happy and to do good while they live. That each of them may eat and drink, and find satisfaction in all their toil—this is the gift of God.* [12]

---

[11] Ecclesiastes 2:24-25
[12] Ecclesiastes 3:12-13

In praise of dogged

Routine is not a word that ever excites us. Perhaps it should. The earth on which we evolved is a planet constant in its habits. It spins so that we are washed alternately and fairly with sunlight and starlight. It orbits the sun so that those of who live outside the tropics experience seasons. It does this again and again and wise organisms fall into step with its quotidienicity. We all know people who get this and are routinely courteous, or hard-working, or thorough or persistently kind. Steady. They are like pillars who hold up the organizations we work in.

Somewhere else in your organization you can probably hear the rodent scurrying of radical upheaval, ambition, people making their mark, all passing by with the lifespan of hamsters while the pillars go on holding up the roof. (I saw a quote: *'Reform! Reform! Aren't things bad enough already?'*)

The odd thing about the steady people is that they don't feel they've achieved anything. All they did was go to work, raise their families, pay their bills; nothing epoch-marking or history-shaping.

But it was good. As the novelist George Elliot wrote at the end of her novel *Middlemarch*:

> *The growing good of the world is partly*
> *dependent on unhistoric acts; and that*
> *things are not so ill with you and me as*
> *they might have been is half owing to the*
> *number who lived faithfully a hidden life,*
> *and rest in unvisited tombs.*

As someone said, 'a small thing is a small thing, but faithfulness in a small thing is a great thing.'[13]

Work and freedom and change

Let's expand this a bit. In its subversive early days, the early church taught that if you could get released from slavery, you should take the chance; life isn't just about being a slave, even if that's all you've known.

This was a first-century germ of a big idea: maybe where you started doesn't have to be where you end. Dream a little. Knead your dreams, work them, in the light of all the constraints on you, and see if you can make something more of your days. There are good reasons for this.

Most of us are rubbish at picking our first jobs. Lots of us do the kind of thing our parents may have done. This has advantages, not least because your parent's experience and network may help you along the way. Doctors breed other doctors, lawyers beget lawyers, office-workers spawn other office-workers, teachers train up little teachers. Presidents raid their networks to insert people in high office. My granny wanted me to be a lawyer. The other side of my family has a lot of accountants. Since accounts freak me out and I can't enjoy the lawyerly habit of writing badly to be legally watertight, neither of these career paths ever appealed. I have been fortunate that an indulgent planet, or an indulgent God and community, allowed me both to be a writer all my life and not to starve.

Lots of today's jobs didn't exist when you were at school. Here's another reason to keep an eye out for a move. I

---

[13] I came across this as from James Hudson Taylor, Victorian founder of the China Inland Mission

went to school in days when schools still employed careers advisors. Mine helped steer me in roughly the right direction. But they didn't tell me about all the jobs that hadn't been invented yet. I enjoyed fruitful years as a freelance writer in the software industry but when I was at school, software wasn't an industry, it was a word you put in inverted commas. My careers teacher, lacking a miraculous ability to predict the future, never opened my eyes to the idea of documenting software, or the roles of web designer or being a social media influencer, or earning money from keep-fit YouTube sessions, or designing virtual fashion for computer game characters. Nor was I advised about already-trodden career paths that would suddenly widen, for example the way government special advisers or Anglican bishops were about to go forth and multiply in the earth. Even my wife, who as a maths teacher *was* expected to go forth and multiply, and divide, and teach others to do likewise, has ended up in a maths-teaching-role and on a career path that didn't exist ten years ago. The world is changing so fast that new jobs are bubbling up all around. So it doesn't harm to expect to move around a little. If you can gain your freedom, don't stay a slave.

The prison of your own making. You can also be enslaved to what you think you should be, or what you think a person like you should be, or what your parents think you should be. Or what you think your parents think you should be. This is a prison of your own making. Don't do it. It's self-harm.

Don't die with your music inside you

That leads us naturally to the idea of vocation. Vocation is about intentionally *not dying with your music still inside you*.

I was very ill when I first came across this thought and it was galvanizing. Since 'galvanizing' means 'using electricity to coat something with zinc', it wasn't *literally* galvanizing, but it was a shaft of sunshine in the forever-January experience of convalescence. Then, and since, the idea of vocation has lit something in me that helped me fight to be well and stay well.

Don't die with your music still inside you. Ask yourself. Other things being equal, feet still roughly on the floor, need for realism acknowledged, what would you love to do? I love asking this question of people. What gives you energy? What is fulfilling? What do you love? What would frustrate you if it were never let out? A famous theologian [14] described vocation as the meeting point between 'your deep gladness' and 'the world's deep need'. Where does that sit for you?

I hesitate to give it an upmarket name like 'vocation' because for some people it means cheerfully and faithfully doing ordinary things. For others, though, it might seem a long way from what they are now and you would never guess it. A person with a career in software wants to turn wood. A researcher would like to be a receptionist in a hospice. Others have found a love of counselling. I know a couple of people who find sanity and happiness through making time to paint. I know that in horrible places of infirmity I have been buoyed by the thought of writing something original, creative and quirky. This is vocation knocking: the chance to take something that belongs to you, and to give it out. Breathe deeply of it, and you oxygenate your soul.

---

[14] Frederick Buechner

Vocation has designed cathedrals that will last a thousand years and spun melodies that the world will sing forever. It has squeezed goodness and grace out of places where only the banal should exist. Vocation is God's fingertips brushing the earth through the actions of people. And when we live out our vocation, we furnish our lives with satisfaction and happiness. Vocation is bread for the hungry soul, a satisfying meal.

I love watching people in their vocation. Someone came to our home to do some carpentry. His first love was restoring antique furniture. His eyes lit on our dining chairs, things that had tumbled to us down through our family as heirlooms. He knew which 19th century decade they were built in and named the style. He told us what he could do to them if he had them in his workshop for a few days.

My son and I both have physics degrees. My physics degree helped me to ascend a few small hills and look up at mountain peaks of human thought. My son, though, climbs these peaks for fun. He knows how partial differential equations work, for example. He understands Maxwell's equations, beautiful things that describe all of classical electromagnetism. I see him in a team experimenting on lone atomic particles that are in near-perfect vacuum and nearly at absolute zero. Even as a child he loved maths problems.

You stumble into vocation all the time. You wander into an office and find people who have time for you and all the resources you need. Someone bakes you a wonderful cake. You see a mum organizing her children or a teacher with her class interested and working hard and happy or arguing furiously with each other about finer points of maths.

Fine, you may say, but a vocation is a bit of a luxury if you're a single parent just holding everything together or someone already buckling under the strain of just earning enough, or you are battling pain and depression, or you are in a toxic workplace, or you are retired. I am not so sure that you are right. For these reasons:

Thinking about vocation at least enables you to set a direction for where you'd like to go and what you'd like to be.

It probably also points to something you're quite good at.

It points you to a higher ambition for your work than just as a vehicle to being solvent or (worse) rich, respected or lauded. These false gods shrivel your soul. Vocation nourishes it.

Even if you don't change career, thinking about the work you love may change how you spend some of the odd scraps of time you already have. If you can't be a professional musician or artist or footballer, be an amateur one. It still will feed your soul. Who knows where these small beginnings will lead? Take a step.

Change to your current circumstances might not be as impossible as you think. If, God forbid, you got a serious illness, or a divorce, you would change things around fast enough. Emails and schedules that tower above you now wouldn't look that way then. They don't matter so much really. The world won't stop even if *you* stop. If you died tomorrow, someone would fix all the emails or finish the jobs. But that thing which is you, that thing you can give to the world, no-one else can do that like you do it.

Negotiate a compromise between vocation and career. This is why artists become graphic designers or would-be session musicians become tutors, or novelists get paid as journalists. Wiggle a little.

Remember life has seasons. The pages turn. Kids grow up. Debts get paid down. The rush to complete qualifications passes. Workplaces change. If your life is a busy river, abuzz with boats and criss-crossed with bridges, so hooting with shipping that you can't take it all in, it may not stay that way. This river will probably evolve into something fat and lazy as it nears the sea, weaving slowly through the bulrushes like a jazz solo. Maybe your vocation awaits a new season. But start it now.

Your vocation is your chance to be big, beautiful you. Do you really want to miss this? So take some steps. Do something. *Do* something. Don't die without giving us a song.

Beware the false gods

Work, that place of so much of our life, is the environment where even atheists worship false gods. Think of the pantheon of them: money, admiration, respect, sex, power, popularity, perfection: we prostrate ourselves before these gods and offer our working lives as sacrifices. This idolatry is everywhere, on every street. I've met people whose career plan was to become a celebrity. We push and exaggerate, some of us lie and cheat, some of us toil away needlessly to serve our false gods. Look at the letters after my name. Look at the sheer amount of *tin* on all my plaques. It's all futile. The gods are false. If you gain the whole world you will lose or destroy yourself. You can also lose or destroy yourself just by *trying and failing* to gain the whole world. Don't do it. Before you smash up the only soul you'll ever have, go back to the real questions. What are you for? What do you love? Who matters to you? That's where the soul-bread is. The false gods can't deliver soul-food; they look like they can, everybody thinks they can, but they can't. Order a pizza from a false god and it will cost you all you have, be cold and soggy, and make you sick.

Work and rest

Rest is woven into good work, part of its fabric. There's an argument that the famous first chapter of the Bible ('let there be light', that stuff) is largely about rest. God sorts through creation, assigning roles to everything, in two lots of three days each. One 'day' he creates sea and sky; in the parallel 'day', half a week later, he populates sea and sky with creatures. And so on. Two lots of three, six days of sort-out, and then the seventh, the climax, the endless day, when God rests.

It can be argued that 'rest' doesn't mean climbing in the divine hammock and putting a good playlist on the holy headphones. Rest means, now that everything's ready, God climbs into his universe and settles there. Rest, then, may be about settling into where you belong: the people you love, the work you love, the rhythms you love. It isn't about leveraging an expensive trip to Disneyland, or buying a long flight to the Maldives, say, in a squalid attempt to pay down the debts of anxiety you have built up over the last several years. It's about taking opportunity as you may to relish and enjoy what you already have, as you go, as you stay in your stride. A psalm expresses much the same thing:

> *Unless the LORD builds the house,*
> *those who build it labour in vain.*
> *Unless the LORD watches over the city,*
> *the watchman stays awake in vain.*
> *² It is in vain that you rise up early*
> *and go late to rest,*
> *eating the bread of anxious toil;*
> *for he gives to his beloved sleep.*
> *³ Behold, children are a heritage from the*
> *LORD,*
> *the fruit of the womb a reward.*
> *⁴ Like arrows in the hand of a warrior*
> *are the children of one's youth.*
> *⁵ Blessed is the man*
> *who fills his quiver with them!*
> *He shall not be put to shame*
> *when he speaks with his enemies in the*
> *gate.* [15]

Among the distilled wisdom in this psalm is the insight that 'anxious toil' doesn't build cities or even cure insomnia. And if you have an overall goal to which you are highly committed (building a safe city, say), it isn't achieved by neglecting everything else. In the psalm, the prime goal is achieved more through the family you raise than the excessive hours you may burn on stone-cutting and watchman-training. It is about not letting work, even vital work, be all-consuming; there's rhythm and rest.

---

[15] Psalm 127 ESV UK.

In case you missed it

So to summarize:

Making is anything that adds to the greater good. And often it serves to pay the bills as well.

Whatever you do, if you do it routinely, faithfully, each day a little better, and thoroughly, just for the sake of doing it well, it will be good for your soul and your happiness and (quite likely) for your career too.

Don't twist or distort work into a pursuit of idols like ambition, wealth, respect, or looking good. None of these gods will satisfy your inner needs and it is entirely possible that the compounding effects of time will expose them, and you, as frauds. Do the making itself, well, for its own sake, and for your soul's.

Be ready to turn the page. Find out what sustains and motivates you, what you love to do, and head for it. Head at a fast pace or a slow one, depending on the constraints on you. Be amateur or professional. Do it as part of your career or outside of it. But at least *start*.

BELIEVING

So far we've said that suffering leads us to focus our energies on *belonging*—strengthening our ties to the networks we value—and *working* or *making* in some role that gives us energy and satisfaction and purpose. Together, these two areas of investment can harness our restless, unsatisfied hearts.

Along the way I've hinted my faith colours all these outlines in; or is the kind of keystone under which everything else fits.

In this fourth movement I want to talk more about this. I don't know where you're starting from, so maybe I should just give you the best eyewitness account I can and you can take it from there.

Who's holding whom

That phrase 'my faith' is familiar enough and helps us get into the discussion, but it isn't really what I mean. It makes 'my faith' sound like some achievement or skill. What I mean, really, is not 'my faith' but 'the fact of God', or maybe just 'God'. God colours all the outlines in. God is the keystone under which everything holds together. 'My faith' is not some mighty grip I have on God but some tender hand he has on me. Think of a father holding a toddler. They are both holding hands, holding each other in love, but one is strong and one is squirmy. One of them has the grip that matters.

And why does he hold me in a tender grip? Because I'm me, so talented, so good, such a dude? No, because he's him. He loves me (I conclude) because he is love. He must feel that way about everyone. In the same way we feel stirrings of love when we see a bad-tempered baby, he feels stirrings of love for us. So that's my first piece of testimony: God is, and God is love. Do I have proof? No, just my shared experience offered to the rest of my network, including you; it's just my personal contribution of subordination and subversion. God is love.

The singularity at the heart of history

My second piece of evidence is Jesus of Nazareth, the one called 'Christ'. This was a person who, on the eye-witness evidence, went around acting like he was God, healing, working miracles, lifting the mask of hypocrisy, kneading the minds of his followers and enlarging their hearts. He is recorded as saying things that are absolutely nuts in anyone else's mouth. (Imagine a politician putting on election posters, 'I am the way, and the truth, and the life.') Then he was brutally executed. And then, as many people testify, he rose from the dead on the following Sunday. Astonishingly, he spent a few more weeks appearing to his followers and teaching them things, before ascending through the dimensions back to God five or six weeks later. Now, his followers argue, he reigns as King.

This raises so many questions probably it is hard to know where to start. A good place, though, is to listen *to what people believe they saw*. This is the raw data. You suspend your critical faculties at first and at least listen. If you don't believe this stuff, others did. And plenty of people, also sound of mind like you, some of them even nearly as smart as you, believed they saw Jesus of Nazareth work miracles, teach, die, rise from the dead, and ascend to heaven. This is the shared understanding of reality that committed Christians hold in common. If you have problems with it, at least respect it and do it the courtesy of understanding it in its own best terms before swatting it away.

Add an obvious but striking fact: Christians don't mark Jesus' tomb, except by opening an empty cave as a tourist attraction.

More circumstantial evidence lies in the enormous appeal of Christianity, with a third of humanity at least notionally within its shadow. As a network of people, the Christian Church has shown resilience through history, a genius for cultural adaption, and has influenced the personal experiences and claims of many more than two billion of our fellow humans.

A lazy explanation for all this is that Christianity is the bad smell that lingers after 500 years of European colonization. That understates the Christian faith today as a worldwide movement, disproportionately strong in Africa, China and Latin America; and it also neglects its long prior history as an Eastern faith.

That bundle of eyewitness observations, and the circumstantial evidence, are, I would like to suggest, like a pea under the mattresses of history, with you being the sleepy princess. Go find the pea. Any number of wonderful discoveries started with people paying attention to rogue data.

Arguments and the pea

Many excellent arguments against the Christian faith are ruffled by a problematic reality: the Christian faith (according to the Christians) is based on an *event*—if you will, 'the Christ event.' It is a brute thing dumped into history. At one level, your opinion doesn't matter: this thing has been dumped into the Universe and if you find that troubling, too bad. Just as if we received what looked like a radio signal from an alien civilisation, and that ruffled everything, it is right that the 'Christ event,' properly understood, disturbs everything. It is a thing that is out there that has happened. So the teachers at your 'Christian' school were bullies and hypocrites? But there was a Christ event. So you prefer a scientific outlook on reality? But there was a Christ event. So you are not a religious type? But there was a Christ event. So you have a problem with a loving God in a suffering world? But there was a Christ event.

At the heart of this rogue data, central to the Christ event, is the resurrection, the idea that the dead Jesus came alive again in a new form and left his tomb, never to die again. It is central, a core understanding that defines the Christian network. If true, nothing ever has been more disruptive or more significant. Alone of all the organized things in the Universe, Jesus overcame the Second Law of Thermodynamics. If Jesus can overcome the Second Law, perhaps in him (as is the claim of Christianity) so can we all. That changes everything.

It has been well pointed out (by someone who is not a Christian interestingly[16]) that the resurrection is not so much a fact of history as a singularity embedded within history. A 'singularity' is an idea borrowed from physics and maths. So-called 'black holes' are singularities. In a singularity, the rules of physics break down. But they are part of the Universe, part of reality. The resurrection is the singularity at the heart of Christianity. It is a part of the Universe, in one sense, but it is where the rules of history, of life and death, have broken down. It is the pea under the mattress. And this is a certain rule on which everyone can agree: if you can't sleep because you need a pea, do something about it.

A relational God

My third claim is that God is relational and known through relationship. This, like everything worth knowing about the Christian faith, can be worked out from the Christ event. (It is also a core belief and claim of the Christian network.) A God who becomes a human, lives in a village for thirty years, and hangs out with friends both before and after his death, is relational. The

---

[16] In his magnificent *History of Christianity* (2009) Professor Diarmaid MacCulloch describes the resurrection as 'beyond the capacity or the intention of the writers to describe it … The New Testament is thus a literature with a blank at its centre; yet this blank is also its intense focus' (p94). MacCulloch describes himself as a 'candid friend of Christianity' who appreciates its seriousness in confronting human suffering but who still lives 'with the puzzle of wondering how something so apparently crazy can be so captivating to millions of other members of our species' (p11).

statement 'God is love,' is meaningless if God isn't relational; love is a verb that requires an object.

The principle of love takes the discussion beyond abstract ideas and puts the matter of knowing and loving God on the same footing as that of growing in friendship or relationship with anyone else. There is a powerlessness at its heart. It is about two would-be friends taking risks to discover intimacy with each other. Again, all this can be derived from the story of Jesus of Nazareth and the eye-witness accounts. He didn't go for spectacular things that might prove he was God and require admiration: leaping off the top of the temple in a single bound, for example. Instead, the miracles he performed were all acts of compassion; though sometimes of anger; and they were about people and their needs. He fed hungry people and physically restored disabled people. And there was a tentativeness about his relationships. If a village didn't want him to come, he went elsewhere. If people begged him to leave their region, he left. His is the behaviour of someone seeking friendship rather than overlordship; the behaviour of someone who values healthy networks and works to nurture them.

Many people miss this gentle note in their understanding of God. One of the problems many of us have against leaning into God for life is that we don't like the thought of it. God might start ordering us around. We might become crazed, or crazy. We resist God because we quite like who and what we are without him. Suitably provoked, we can raise all kinds of fine-sounding objections but our main reason for resisting God is a simple blank refusal to go there.

On our evidence Jesus seemed, at one level, fine with that, in that he moved on rather than blasting people with a thunderbolt. On another level, though, once your proud heart has been dismantled by his tender love, once his fierceness and gentleness has remade you as a human, obedience is less of a problem. Melted chocolate can be poured into a million shapes. Cold chocolate just snaps.

The missing something

A lot of us know we are missing something. Are you missing something? Even in all the good things about you that your loved ones will mention at your funeral, are you missing something?

My testimony is that there are loose threads in our lives that if we trace them to their source, lead to God. This is unsurprising to the Christian, since we are inheritors of a shared story that humanity's biggest problem is a ruptured relationship with our Creator. No wonder, then, there are loose threads; no wonder there are missing somethings.

I have met people who find one end of a thread of transcendence in their lives but haven't found the other end. They seek it in music or in nature, for example. Some just get misty-eyed and sentimental. The writer Terry Pratchett had a transcendent encounter with an orang utan once [17]—I am not joking, they stood, unblinking looking at each other—and when dying of Alzheimer's,

---

[17] The orang's name was Kusasi, and diligent searching on the Internet might reveal more of this story. Pratchett's Discworld character of the Unseen University's Librarian is the greatest orang utan in fiction (in my opinion, but it's a thin field).

he went all the way back to East Asia in a doomed attempt to find the orang again. Terry Pratchett is a hero of mine, a writer's writer. But you can do better than locking eyes with an orang utan across a crowded jungle. I hope he did.

Others tug at loose threads in their lives by seeking harmony, or peace, or mathematical elegance, or love. Science, I have often thought, is driven by a love of beauty as much as by curiosity or by a desire to serve the common good. The Cavendish Laboratory in my hometown of Cambridge, whose toiling inmates have earned thirty Nobel Prizes as of 2019, has a text written on the old front door, put there by James Clerk Maxwell: 'The works of the Lord are great, sought out of all of them that have pleasure therein.' Open the doors to the Cavendish, he was saying, and through physics, seek pleasure, and seek God.

In the previous century, the philosopher Bertrand Russell was a famous atheist, even writing a book entitled *Why I am not a Christian*. But there are other sides to his story. Russell's daughter, Katherine Tait, said of him: 'Somewhere at the back of my father's mind, at the bottom of his heart, in the depths of his soul, there was an empty space that had once been filled by God, and he never found anything else to put in it.' Russell was now haunted by a 'ghost-like feeling of not belonging in this world.'

Russell himself wrote in a private letter, 'The centre of me is always and eternally a terrible pain . . . a searching for something beyond what the world contains, something transfigured and infinite – the beatific vision, God – I do not find it, I do not think it is to be found – but the love of it is my life . . . it is the actual spring of life within me.'[18]

Look again at the main theme of the book, how suffering turns to rubble much of what we thought was good and reveals the main themes of life as networking and vocation, belonging and making. I have come to believe that these can only be fully worked out in relationship with God and his purposes. Their appearance in our lives without God is more like us hearing a melody on the wind, rather than getting the full symphony. They are the smell of baking bread, and they should put us on the hunt for the full loaf. We can work this out a bit more.

Networking

The appearance of Christ disrupted many things, and not least Jewish theology. For most of two thousand years, the Jewish people had come to understand that (a) they were God's people and (b) God was one, and so worshipping many gods was a bad idea. Jesus disrupted this simple idea by behaving like God on earth, while at the same time praying to God in heaven. How many gods were there now?

The new discipline of Christian theology took several centuries to get to a settled view of this, though the main themes were obvious from the beginning. Putting them in legal language was difficult. Along the way things got

---

[18] Both these Russell quotes were dug out by Prof. Alister McGrath and referenced in his Gresham College lecture *Why God Won't Go Away*. Gresham College lectures can be accessed from their website. 'Three brains' McGrath has doctorates in biophysics, divinity, and intellectual history.

tribal and political, with rival theological camps fighting in the streets at times like football fans.

The problem was really that God was Three as well as One, or he was One with a certain Threeness: Father, Son, and the 'Holy Spirit'. (The Holy Spirit is the one whom Jesus promised to send as a kind of mentor to the church after he left. Another writer, Bernard of Clairvaux, called the Holy Spirit 'God's kiss'.) Human language was not built for this stuff and it is not surprising that it led to fights.

In this theological and linguistic jumble, many people struggled to find a description of God that described God as one; and God as Father, Son and Holy Spirit; and didn't lead, metaphorically, to your car getting its windscreen smashed by theological rivals. One fruitful suggestion was a newly coined Greek word, *perichoresis*. *Peri* is to do with around and about (hence *perimeter*), *choresis* is to do with space and hence with movement across space. *Perichoresis* is thus a kind of rotation, or a jazz trio, with Father, Son and Spirit, each of whom is fully God, collectively loving and contributing. In this picture God is himself a network, an intermingled set of loving relationships that collectively is one Being.

I'm sorry for the excursion into what I think is known as Patristic Theology but it floods our subject with light. *God is a perichoresis*, a dance, a trio. No wonder then that his Universe is a perichoresis. No wonder that networks are everywhere: a proton a network of quarks and gluons; an atom a network of leptons and baryons; a human unit not an individual woman or man but a network—a marriage and a home and children, a family. *Male and female created he them*. In this Universe—this perichoretic

Universe—everything relates with everything else, one distended, intricate network, threaded through geological ages. We are what we are because earlier stars blew up and created the heavy elements. We are what we are because our great-grandparents met. We are what we are because the networks into which we are born shape us. Is it genes or environment than shape us? It is both, it is the *perichoresis* of the Universe that was spun out of the *perichoresis* of God.

So beautiful. So terrible, incidentally, when human beings become network abusers and network drainers. On the other hand: no wonder networks enliven us and give us meaning. We were made by them and through them and for them.

Vocation and story

If networking and belonging has its origin in what God *is*, vocation or making is found in God's *purpose*. This is, on the face of it, unexpected. How can God have a purpose? How can God be said to be working towards something? Does that not mean he is therefore less than all sufficiently himself now and therefore, perhaps, not God at all?

The answer to this, I think, is that God is love, and it is the nature of love to create, nurture and fulfil. You can't be love without some expression of your love being worked out. Arguably then it is the nature of God to kiss dust and make souls and get involved in their growing up.

If God is love, then necessarily there is not only an object involved. There is also a story, a love story. Love requires a story, I think. So is the Universe a love story? Is our personal story a little plot line within this greater story? Let's explore this a bit.

Story

One obvious observation about humans is that we are built out of stories. What is the story of your life, your country, your plans, your future? Who are you? Why are you who you are? I think your answers, probably, would be stories. We think we understand something if we grasp its story. I know how an internal combustion engine works, at least to a certain level, if I understand the repeating story of what happens inside it. How many stories will you hear today? How many will you tell? Reporters pursue 'the story'; children love a story; audiences stir a little when you start to tell a story. When you tell your spouse what kind of day you had, I think it will involve stories. We eat carbon in various forms because we're made of carbon; we devour stories because we're made of them.

The Christian faith is a story, indeed an overarching story, a universal story. It is also a love story. How does it work when tested against reality? And is it a story within which I can locate my personal story? I hope I have made my biases clear, but let's look.

The Christian story

The Christian story is (as we have seen) about God creating a Universe and creating creatures with whom he intends to dwell and whom he intends to thrive. Then, it's about a human-led break with God, our own Independence Day. Ever felt God is distant? Ever felt alienated? According to the Christian story, that curious sense of alienation is because we *are* alienated—from God and each other.

Then the story is about God coming to our rescue, but coming alone, unarmed, without a bodyguard, as a baby, growing up to become a young Messiah. The life, suffering, death, resurrection and ascension of Jesus Christ brings God's character, intent, and capability to us in digestible human form. Jesus does not so much make his way in the world, as make a way *for* the world, a way back to God through himself.

Installed in heaven as King, he sends the Holy Spirit into his followers and the story continues. People turn to God through Christ and form a network together. This network grows through the world, and through history. The network, the church, and the rule of God it tries to live out, is a kind of foretaste, indeed a spoiler, of the end. The end is re-creation and re-unification with God through Jesus. The part now is an early spillage of eternity into time. Signs of this early spillage are peace with God, reconciled and reconstructed lives and relationships, the flow of justice, and the healing and fulfilling of creation through the practice of vocation. Several things are remarkable about how this is happening:

It is designed to spread, like yeast through flour, or like an infection through a body.

It is human-scale yet capable of reaching all humanity.

It infuses everything Christians do with direction and purpose. To follow Christ is to be a harbinger, a disrupter, a peacemaker and a patient revolutionary. With everything we touch—our work, our play our networks—

we foreshadow a day when God, people and creation cooperate and thrive together in harmony. We overturn the dead old order with subordination, subversion, faith, hope and love.

And yet it doesn't work

Yet it doesn't work. Christians are familiar with their efforts being internally compromised, being found insufficient to the task, and then disintegrating. Like Jesus' life from some perspectives, they look like things started OK but never worked out. We've had 2000 years and haven't set the world right or brought in the Kingdom of God. To be a Christian, it would seem, is to commit to playing on the losing side of history. The end of all our striving is weakness and loss. We bloom for a while, and then the flowers fall.

Here we perhaps come to the greatest feature of the Christian Church, one largely acknowledged by the outside world but largely neglected by the Christians. *We are not very good.* Back in the 13th century, that charismatic leader Francis of Assisi formed a missionary order devoted to serving others out of great personal poverty and he was wise enough to call them the 'Order of the Little Brothers.' Still today, Franciscans can put the letters OFM after their names, which is the Latin equivalent, *Ordo Fratrem Minorum*. (In England the Franciscans were known as the Greyfriars because of the rough clothing they wore.)

Just a few years later, the Spaniard Dominic founded another order, the Order of Preachers (OP), dedicated to learning and instructing the masses. (These were the Blackfriars, because they put a black cowl over their head to show they meant business.)

Possibly the church's worst failing is that too many of us, as it were, join the Order of Preachers and too few of us admit to really belonging to the Order of the Little Brothers—instructing people in the right being generally more appealing to the human ego then embracing poverty, obscurity and loss.

And yet in doing this, we are neglecting our superpower, which is that the weak, the lost, the sad, the defeated and the small, so long as they faithfully cling to God, are the bells through whom the forward echoes of the resurrection power of God will clang. *Blessed are the poor in spirit, for theirs is the Kingdom of God.*

We should know better. How did Jesus die? Naked, nailed up, spat upon and with his critics rubbing their hands and cracking their knuckles in glee. That was Friday. What happened on Sunday? He walked out of his tomb and made one of his best friends, a young woman, jump, by looking her in the face and speaking her name. Then probably her mascara ran—certainly *she* ran—as she laughed and cried at the same time.

We Christians are born to hum a tune, be overwhelmed and defeated, and be buried, but leave something of the Kingdom of God behind us. The stone the builders rejected becomes the cornerstone. The buried seed precedes the harvest. Whatever joy, beauty, service, love and truth we deposit in the world are little hints of a better day. God in resurrection power, through those bones, will do the rest.

The Christian hope is to sing for a while, dance for a while, suggest a better day, and then to be buried with our hopes unfulfilled while the world stomps on, passing our graves. Our service in the world is, or should be, marked with love, faith—and hope. We are the order of the little brothers. Don't look to us to bring the revolution. Watch us serve and die, but then watch God bring the rebirth of the whole cosmos, in justice, and goodness, and newness, and thriving, and peace.

At its best, then, the Church is God's hint, God clearing his throat, God tuning his trumpet. Here in Cambridge, for example, my own church for several decades ran a day centre for old people and a house that provided care in the community for people with learning difficulties. Half the homeless provision in our city is Christian-inspired. Also in the city is a nationally admired Christian-led centre for children and families. Just outside the city is a facility that provides work, accommodation and friendship for men who have probably tangled with the law and are difficult to house anywhere else. I could go on for a long time. Quite a lot that softens our city, that fights injustice, that extends provision beyond government programmes, that splashes grace around, is inspired by the Christian faith, and is a sort of harbinger or hint of a much greater and just world to come.

This stuff resonates and gets amplified through society when people who are not part of the Christian story pick up on it and own it for themselves and spread it too. Integrity and respect and social justice and cooperation can flow through networks just like anything else. People who would not claim much by way of Christian faith can be found living and fighting for a better day. They are working for the kingdom of God, if they knew, doing justice and exercising kindness and hatching beauty. Some were inspired by Christian examples, some came up with things themselves. They know what they are doing is good. They don't necessarily know that it is good because they have trimmed their sails to the breeze from God. Reality is pushing into *their* stories. They are finding that they are working with the grain of the world.

Hence vocation. When each of us gets to be and do what we were made to be and do, we are dipping our feet in the longer and larger remaking of Creation.

Truly God is in this place, and we know it not. As a Christian believer, who stumbled into the Christian faith and got stuck there without deserving any of it, I see God's work all around me in people I admire and love, who may not realize what they are doing, what breeze is filling their sail.

And remember the powerlessness here. It remains a strength. The Kingdom of God is benchmarked not by conquests duly hailed but by love expressed. We can't do the kingdom, the re-creation that's needed. We can't even get our own lives together. All we can do is work and play and love in the light of hope and keep turning back to God. Our lives are a *perichoresis*, an improvisation for God in the warming day. We can't make a new world. But we can do our making together, in the light of God's remaking of us, in gratitude, with all our energy and skill, and as a foretaste of his greater remaking to come. For me, belonging and vocation light us up because they work, they are the foundation of a happy life. They are discovered through living. They are the grain of the universe. They are lit with the light of God.

And they are just the start.

ABOUT THIS BOOK

The copy in your hands is a so-called Advanced Review Copy which (I hope) has come to you free of charge. The final published book is available to order or pre-order via your favourite outlets.

I would greatly welcome any comments, either to me personally via my website glennmyers.info, or by putting a review up somewhere. I enjoy being encouraged and appreciate being criticized. Public comment is a currency of the Internet and honest reviews can help enormously. Thanks.

* * *

Many thanks to my beta readers, Matthew Philip, Malcolm Wylie and Andrew Chamberlain

My friend and colleague Chris Lawrence created the cover with skill and generosity.

I'm very happy to be in touch further. You can contact me via my website:

Glennmyers.info

Or my blog on things slow
Slowmission.com

I'm also (in an out of touch, fogeyish way) on Goodreads, Twitter and Facebook.

OTHER BOOKS

More than bananas

How the Christian faith works for me and the whole Universe

More than Bananas is a companion piece to *Bread*, an earlier mix of experience and reflection. I wrote it while recuperating from my coma. If *Bread* is my exploration of the question 'what is the point?' *More than Bananas* is an attempt at the question, 'is Christianity true?' For brief and flukish moments, and principally because the Kindle and epub versions were free for a time, *More than Bananas* has been a global theology bestseller.

I also write comic fiction. Here I'm also exploring the wonderful regions between faith and doubt, this time by picturing the unseen world all around us and imagining that world as a shoddy realm of thwarted hopes, existential doubt, backstabbing, spirits, souls and sales conferences.

If you want to know why I write so feelingly about failure and disappointment, much of that comes from not having these books published by a reputable publisher. My solution was to form a disreputable publisher and publish them myself. They are my favourites out of all my books. The first book in the series can be downloaded onto your phone for free. My cunning plan, borrowed from the world of drug dealing, is that you get addicted and start spending money on further doses.

Paradise: a divine comedy
You think you've got problems.

My favourite restaurant closed down. My girlfriend left. A bad-tempered lawyer named Keziah crashed her car into mine. And we couldn't even die properly.

Paradise for us turned out to be a cage in the heavens where evil spirits market-tested new temptations, where everyone could see our memories, and where we were stuck forever.

A snake with a personality disorder offered us a way out. The trouble was, it meant facing up to the worst problem of all: Myself.

Paradise—a divine comedy is a disorderly romp through death, life, good food and redemption.

Paperback ISBN 978-0-9565010-0-4
Ebook ISBN 978-1-4523-8994-3

I won this book from the site and absolutely loved it. A hysterical surrealist take on what is out there after life on earth, or next to life on earth, or simultaneous with life on earth, or whatever. A story of Gods in kilts, crystal clear memories, and walls made of our pixelated fears. Delightful. (4 stars) Jeannette M, Goodreads

I also won Paradise in the goodreads competition…and I am really glad that I did. I didn't love the first chapter since it threw a bit too much weird at you all at once (penguins which pull your soul around are an example). After that, the story got going and was really enjoyable! Sometimes you want to hit the main character on the back of the head and tell him to stop being a wuss, but how would you react if you had to build a paradise controlled by some used-car-salesman-style gods? If you like quirky and surreal stories about the afterlife, then I would highly recommend Paradise. (4 stars) Katie Webb, Goodreads

A superb rollercoaster of a story; loved every minute! Phil Groom of the Christian Bookshops Blog

So hilariously funny! I've already started reading the next one. I would highly recommend this to just about anyone.' (five stars) Stewartc85 on Goodreads

What a great book! Loved the characters, the creativity, the dialogue, the imaginative idea of evil spirits keeping humans as pets, the insightful lines: 'a creative, radical thinker, but not a creative, radical doer', for one example; the image of the rain of God's mercy, …. There is much to think about beyond the story itself and the book gives a delightfully comic but definitely insightful look into the human psyche and soul. It's a mark of a good book (for me, at least) when I look forward to picking it up again to read and am slow to put it down. I loved every aspect of it. I was given Paradise by a friend who knows I enjoy good writing. I have to say that any book which keeps me reading the next chapter because I've become absorbed in the characters and the unfolding story is a book well worth reading. This is one of those books. I look forward to the sequel. (4 stars) S Sutton, Amazon.com

Loved the plot, the characters, the dialogue, the pace, the suspense, the surprises, the imagery, the metaphors, the depth, and the meaning. And I laughed a lot. It is really wonderful. Kenny Parker, Amazon.co.uk

The Wheels of the World

Thanks to a near-death experience, Jamie Smith can commute between earth and the heavens, where souls swim, ideas grow and improbable dollops of joy fall through the sky.

Jamie and his scary colleague Keziah have been recruited into an eccentric organization that tries to fix broken souls and change the course of history. Which is fine, except Jamie isn't too sure about the health of his own soul—and definitely doesn't want to find out.

He'd rather be working for The Department, the heavenly bureaucracy that plans the future universe and offers a 30-hour working week, enviable employee benefits, and a tennis-skirted line manager named Anna-Natasha.

As Jamie's problems mount, dark forces close in, and time runs out, he's left with a decision: if he's fleeing from himself, which way should he run?

The Wheels of the World, *sequel to* Paradise: a divine comedy *is a comedy about how we change on the inside.*

Paperback ISBN 978-0-9565010-1-1
Ebook ISBN 978-0-9565010-2-8

Brilliant continuation of the first book, I enjoyed the style and characters as well as the quirky look at life/death and everything in between. Could it really be so??! Eagerly awaiting the next book! – from Amazon

The Sump of Lost Dreams

Thanks to a near-death experience, Jamie Smith can commute across dimensions to the heavens, home of the invisible machinery behind our world.

Along with his scary colleague Keziah Mordant, he has been recruited into an eccentric organization that tries to change things on earth by fixing and steering broken souls through the many hazards of the heavens: bad moods, clouds of anxiety, vortexes of self-loathing.

Mark Bright, Keziah's delicious new boyfriend, is trying to set up a cafe and homelessness hub on earth. In the heavens, evil spirits plot to destroy it, and at the same time plot to send Jamie and Keziah into the celestial sewer system, The Sump of Lost Dreams.

Helped in the battle by the prophet Jonah and an ancient female

physicist, Jamie and Keziah visit the souls of two town planners, patch up some old sinners, try to outwit some very stupid beings, fight each other, a lot, and even argue with the Personification of Divine Wisdom.

Along the way, Keziah fears being found out by happiness and Jamie goes on a circular tour of the foods of Southeast Asia.

The Sump of Lost Dreams *is about when you think you've lost everything, you might be right.*

Paperback ISBN 978-0-9565010-3-5
Ebook ISBN 978-0-9565010-4-2

Glenn Myers channels Terry Pratchett, Douglas Adams and John Bunyan in his writing - very entertaining and thought provoking. Did you ever wonder if you had a soul and what it might look like?

Welcome to a world, or rather a metaphysical space, where souls may get over-run with idealised memories or ravaged by civil war between yourself and your dark alter ego, you know the part of your psyche with the attitude and massive AK47. A place where Depression really is a Black Dog sniffing around, along with his pals Lust, Anger and Contempt. They have plans to shape this metaphysical space, and the souls within it - Jamie Smith is the flawed 'hero' who, along with his co-workers, has other plans for this same space... conflict ensues, one that draws you in and keeps you guessing.

An enjoyable story which weaves together events and intentions in the heavenlies with happenings on earth. No need to fear any black and white moralising, Myers' characters and environment are too complex and his writing is too intelligent for that. Recommended- along with the rest of the trilogy. Helen – Goodreads.

Lightning Source UK Ltd.
Milton Keynes UK
UKHW040628251121
394565UK00001B/77